UNDERSHORE

Kelly Hoffer

UNDERSHORE

Kelly Hoffer

LIGHTSCATTER
PRESS

Printed in the United States of America

Cover art: Laminaria Bulbosa cyanotype print from *Photographs of British Algae: Cyanotype Impressions* (1850) by Anna Atkins. Original from the New York Public Library. Image ID: 419532.

Cover design: Kayden B. Groves and Jem Ashton

Interior design: Jem Ashton

Author photo credit: Kelly Hoffer

Lightscatter Press is an independent nonprofit literary press with 501(c)(3) tax-exempt status that seeks to preserve and extend the material, tactile experience of the printed, bound text through beautiful, innovative design that integrates digital artifacts and experiences created for and with the printed text. Our home is Salt Lake City, Utah.

Library of Congress Control Number: 2023930819
Names: Hoffer, Kelly, Author
Title: Undershore, Poems by Kelly Hoffer
Description: Salt Lake City, Lightscatter Press (2023)
Identifiers: Library of Congress Control Number: 2023930819 | ISBN: 978-1-7364835-2-7 (trade paperback)
LC record available at https://lccn.loc.gov/2023930819

First printing

Lightscatter Press
Salt Lake City, Utah
www.lightscatterpress.org

Contents

'A KNOT DENSE AND BEAUTIFUL'

Cloth—as clothing, as household artifact—is "fragile and transient," embodying "ideas concerned with the reiterative and degenerative processes of life… witness[ing] routines, rituals and intimacies" (Caroline Bartlett, textile artist). When you encounter a QR code on the pages of this book, scan it with your camera phone to be taken to a cyanotype quilt containing audio recordings of the poet reading the poems. The quilt will also offer you multiple thematic "threads" to follow, allowing you to arrange the sequence of the poems in a new way each time you read.

For another material 're-gesturing' of these poems, visit the digital gallery of 'a knot dense and beautiful,' a textile book made in response to *Undershore*, made by textile artist Lauren Callis.

Foreword by Diana Khoi Nguyen

undershore, *v. trans.* To prop up; to support or strengthen with shore.
    fig. To support, strengthen, sustain

Undershore is incandescent, like an electric light housing a filament which glows when a current passes through it. A filament as tender and tenacious as spider silk weathering the elements. Its lyrical adroitness is immediately felt and heard.

Here is a sweeping field of vision which captures both horizontal and vertical planes of the earth: from cumulonimbus clouds to what arrives with the tide, to roots deep in dirt and the lingering presence of loved ones. From its opening lines, the speaker situates us in earthly space: "We are walking down a ledge and then there is no place out / but up. We are above water." In the poems that gracefully follow, we traverse the meticulous ledges and edges of a heightened poetics of grief. Through the speaker's navigation and keen sense for wonder, we float through sky and sea into realms of loss, memory, desire, anxiety–and are never adrift; remarkably in the aftermath of a parental death, there is eros, not erosion.

Central to the textual variations of this collection are the suite of "Visitation" poems which chart the speaker's encounters with a deceased mother's memory, presence, and haunting. Some of these poems drift across the page, while others anchor in place via intimate prose blocks which eschew visual accessibility. Dispersed like seeds via wind and animal carriage are artful catalogs, lists, an abecedarian, floral translations and transmutations, and rhapsodic engagements with the dictionary in which words like "pile" or "list" prompt playful meditations on how objects and anatomy from the observable world formulate integral rhythms and routines which make up the ecosystem of all living and nonliving entities. As one poem title aptly captures one core through-line of thought: "All movement mimics movement."

The objective correlative of this collection encompasses much of the floral and natural world, yielding sites of transcendent linguistic turns. After a death comes a "disrupted texture," but in mapping the body with the natural world, the speaker finds a way to move forward, as clouds are never not moving, as plants continue to grow toward the sun, until the day that they don't. Never will I forget this speaker: "try to shape my mouth a poppy / ringed with dew, my neck a greening nape. I come / off inelegant–something borrowed, something / burrowed. unseemly. lustering." Yet in these vulnerable admissions of self, and statements of sheer longing, the poet's sightline is unerringly honest, seeking, and true.

VISITATION

We are walking down a ledge and then there is no place out but up. We are above water. It is noon-time. It is not cold, but I know we are somewhere thin. The quiet houses wait for us on the ridge. The path narrows. The path is a tree. A white tree. The bark is not white, but the wood so worn and eaten it has become white. Bleached by something I can't touch or name. I don't think you can climb it. I tell you so. I don't tell you that I am scared of it also. Mother, I fear falling. I wince to see you crouch, trying to scale the trunk. I stop you. There is no leaving here. This is the end. We make a hole at the base of the tree and fill it with our bodies. You hold me again. Your whole body a vessel for me one more time. We take comfort in each other, side by side, sipping warmth.

HYACINTH

Hyacinth is two faces of unequal blush turned away from each other

hyacinth is a stone that is red orange, is a flower that is blue purple

hyacinth is a color that is either red orange or blue purple

hyacinth is a bulbous plant native to Turkey, Lebanon, and Iran

is composed of modular star flowers pinned too close together to suit a metaphor of petalled constellations

each flower is a word permuted, petals chosen, with sense in mind—chain, chin, hint, hitch, yacht, inch

is fashionable in the 18th century, 2000 Dutch-processed cultivars

is so numerous, blossoms drip from wooden ships and petals accrete between the wax-paper lining of chocolate boxes

is a cluster of fraying floss poked through by a spike, its color is cotton candy melted to viscous sugar, strand

is a difficult flower to dry, the cone shape requires disassembling before pressing to one plane between papers, parting the flowers like curls on a head, a tender scalp shines through

is a man named for a flower died flowerlike

is a lover of Apollo, coveted by Zephyrus, a man (so young still, all of him a candle pulled from wax, smooth and un-calloused, still cooling) caught in the ravage of a jealous wind, died as a flower, the neck one of many clipped stems

a disrupted texture

unearthing *cinch* if you are loose with your c's, *acid* if you let t's slip to d's, or *akin*, if the c become k, *tith* is not a word, nor is it contained in hyacinth, but it should be both—a harvest with something left out, a synonym for gleaning

stone facets decoupaged in sculptured tissues, petals translucent with the application of paste

the distinct hue of each varietal carries its own scent

devout repetition dissolving to sound

15

hyacinth, hi-a-sin-th is (in syllables) a greeting to a little sin caught in my teeth

is the asymmetry of the face of my beloved, freshly shaven, pieces of cotton tacked to the clumsy places, hy-a-cinth

I WANT ABYSSES

the dove winding outward via sky
a profile, a blackening eagle, a sparrow
wings eyed from underneath lose
their color

if I dive into water between
cliffed ledges and move
toward the ever-approaching, ever-darkening
darkness, only to turn
around and look above
me. I dove and I saw the sky
the same as before
my sounding. the sky the truer
        unchanging from
differing depths, the sky the truer
deep, masked by the bending of true
cyan, and I can see nothing
of the stars
or of the voids between them as I am
saturated by light—
it takes my vision
away from, its brightness blots out the
blackness of, my sight, I
don't know where to encounter the blue
or if I could if I would, a sheet of it
painted on celestial film and the dove
remains   a hovering
void in the void
through it I see the abyss
the desire I desire

A WINTER SAMPLER

wood takes a suede edge
frost builds on the lip

crystal accreting
crystal to hived print

I approach the water,
find iced moss, fringes
brushed silver in paint

rust blooms through algae
sits cloud on limpid
mineral, pressing—

gather needles in
gardens, as glow worms
sprout to a chain from

unprecious metals
the bark leafs off, falls
like lead flaked, adorns
the shallow basin

tittering, the trees
rest their limbs, heavy
on the ground and guard
space for coming gold

morning on the frayed
strings between branches
white silk spilled in bells
the snow settles sound
let us collect, leave

the small hearts of beech
in kindling baskets
they're for burning—rest,

bask doleful, alive
in the warmth from cut
stone, coal slid to rock
glass obsidian
candy she brought me

to know seeds pried from
wrought material,
mark on silt paper
may we ask, in time,
for new permission?

the air comes in cusps
my mouth shapes an o
breathes out cradle cut,
the new resin sly
on the sugar, bit

between bitter and
salted lips and tongue
if we taste it, tap
upon cube, piles
of translucent sweet

carated fruits, how
jewels take color—
I wrap clementines
in red cellophane
for her winter gift.

I CANNOT LIVE WITH YOU

I approach you in a hallway.
you are well dressed.
you tell me the distance between a crane's bill and a geranium.
the distance is New Zealand.

I approach you in a hallway. you are wearing
a purple shirt with checks. you tell me
the difference between my joy and our life. I don't want
it in my house.

the hallway has windows. raging. the weather
is seizing in the window and the wall next to the window
is white paint. is calm.

I approach you in the hallway and I tell you the difference
between your shirt and the calmness of white paint.

the tide is flecked with sand and it looks
like gold iridescing in a dust as the water comes in.

you approach me in the hallway and I am glad
for the quiet of your entrance. I tell you
there has been an error.

the depth of your hair and the shirt
you left in the bathroom that is filled with
the depth of your smell of
a kind. the private direction. up and left.

boxes robed in white paint. a liquid separating
from the contained particulate. you have been always
so particular in your shirts. the box is
particular in its directions.

I approach for the steadiness of a hand.
I missed you this morning in my way
of moving outward toward the ocean.

I tell you the time for arrangement is soon. I approach
a mussel, opening the shell to show the ridges of
its dog-lips. there is a peacrab, small and whole,
feeding from its gills.

SOUND (SWIMMING)

you wave goodbye in the water   I wave   hello

in my hand   in my

water is marred by   shape the shape of   my hand

in a pulsing shallow   my-very-own

form. mar is water when   I feel it

vapor rises clean   off the body   rising

out of liquid, brushing a   distinct

temperature as yesterday's   sun radiates in

my-very-own chest   but a lingering

bloom of cold on the legs

the lake reeds swaying

under me, but

not   very, the small movement

LASH

You left me in a dream. The place I go to leave you. You left and when I woke to ask for comfort, you didn't. It's been a moment now in this shade that we make. The begonia split six times. Flowered thrice. The while building. My body keeps eggs for us, and I keep discarding. To think of how to last I think of the last thing. Palm shadows on a carpeted desert before the grand dissolution. I am disappointed by our last kiss. The one before you left me. There was no tongue in it even if it was velvet. I could taste the cloth you bit it with. If our mothers are ghosts, yours is older. I imagine her leading mine along by the hand, the two tethered just to each other by a single blond string. Balloons float up into a windless cloudscape. When my mother was young, her hair was the wet black of a seal. A dream is lipped and silver. Like a fishknife. She is pressing into her life after life. Gray paint on top of gray canvas, wafer-thin. I am learning about doubt, the depth I can cut to. The sound keeps filling. The well the walls cave in on in unimpeded motion.

newly, truly, bluely ever madly, sadly,
blue blue blue, raw and bluely
piece of meat, awfully raw and
tender. tenderly. ready for the swoon to fool
me, dropped into a pool of cooling
lust. or a sentence seamed with stitching
nectar. bitten full of pollen. bees sip from
the mottled fool of me, even as a flower spools
sweet things beside. necked and fought, came
by myself. nursing a bitter back
of the throat. try to shape my mouth a poppy
ringed with dew, my neck a greening nape. I come
off inelegant—something borrowed, something
burrowed. unseemly. lustering. laying my pleasure across
the bed, if I give you a phrase will you sup-
ply the subject, if I tell   the moon
a phase will she bring me a spot
of light to hang among my singly, madly, deepening
blue.

as in, I am found
wanting in that
abyssal way
of having none as

in they are not
in me, a me made virtual, a
whole

this abrupt extrusion
depths wanting
promontorypromontorypromontory

VISITATION

in the corner a woman's face
           abandons its sharpness

     the light on her glasses

she flits away from my
eager hands

     floating through contour

conversations
with my mother, her face obscured,
her breath turning
milky, opaque enough to hide her
eyelashes.

       When she
was dying, reduced
to a state of yes and no, there were
no more words, she told me
with her eyes, syntax beads
unstringing, replacing
each of my sounds
with a darkening iris, the slighting
dilation between thoughts   where is she   drifting
in my white or is she   just
the darkness
a shadow on shadow, a place my mind
blotted out
in the recess of the sun.

CATARACT

from the French, from the Latin, from the Greek
"a down rushing bird"

the initial cataract$_1$ was the flood-
gate of heaven, a structure intended   to keep the rain back. holding water
in the sky preserves the land as land. this is   the defense of the desert
against the creeping   sea.
a flood is a body   of water moving to its improper place is
a state of swelling is the improper   expansion of such a body. the cataract$_2$
becomes the waterfall, the precise escape of the liquid
the wall of its name was meant to keep, as it has always
rained, the breach is implied.   the water must fall   headlong
as in, without obstacle. "headlong" to mean with break-neck
speed. your head is not safe
in a cataract$_2$. the interruption of rocks
or earth births a cascade. the cascade is a diminutive
fall. light cascades through a window grate, another cataract$_3$,
to be considered, that mesh over the opening of a building. a portcullis,
named cataract$_4$ for the liquid slipping of its spikes into ground,
its motion that of the cataract$_2$ the cataract$_1$
stilled. a cervical stitch keeps a body within a body, the cataract$_4$ keeps
a flood of people unrealized.   I am too
afraid of the ledge of my brain.   the cataract$_5$ of the eye turns
light to liquid.   clouded.   bright.   the mote dehisces to release an atmosphere, the
blindness unlocatable.   this cloud accompanied
me from the floodgates of heaven, and I find
all the cataracts$_{12345}$ are clouds,   in the sky, on the lens, of the mist rising
as water hits yet another water, making figures out of air. a cataract is a cloud moving
with uncanny speed. the marbler combs his pigments, brings the pattern
out with a sheet hovering over a pool. here is the ledge.
here is the margin. under a still sky, the glass
flowers of the desert, filled as they are with bladders
of air, float on the floodtide, the clink of glass on glass re-sounding
upon each of their meetings at the surface of the water

WORRY

v. transferred.　To bite at or upon (an object);
to kiss or hug vehemently;
to utter (one's words) with the teeth nearly closed, as if biting or champing them.

stormy searing　　roof of the mouth　　labile bilious　　are you all of your toomuchness?

I hold my excess out before me and　ask about its day　　latinate emotions feigning a body ride in on a flood

a fickleness so convincing　I swear it is rooted　　existing continues

to be my pre-condition　　even as I smother my muscular wit　　in a washed-out basin

tarrying with the rigid strands　my mother's lungs never would have survived

this twenty-twenty　breathing disease　　I worry　about her ghost making it through　　coated in powder

shifty wave in shifting light　I worry　　(on the scale of the

third or thirtieth time)　about which infirmities follow　us into our afterlives　　which is to say

which shades　　follow us into the minds　　of other people　　I can attest

that you don't stop worrying your sick mother after she dies

this is not the first time I have thought　　of where to put down my veil of hair

the magi gift I want to make of it　　a Victorian keepsake kept between teeth

bent on breaking　　piled in a　　homely settlement

COMING NIGH ON EVE

brightening desire pokes heat
pronged furl   shoot
kernels hitting a bowl
pushed over, a wave
accrual threading an eye (want
and I want and I want)
eating all the fruits, lick'em to pits
stones in my middles
shaved skin from a ruby a
liquid stilled and sunned
in, spit shone, cleaned to facets
a smooth plane shows me mine,
well, basin—concave placed, carving
a countenance (wait while I count)
out the syllables tra la tra la sings
my face, my name
a flecked mineral hushed to a corner
it's a stumbling heat in winter
(you told me to) make birds with my hands
hover and bite this
breath on snow unlit
bodies (all the sex
I am not having all the sex
that I am)
imaginings in the egress
(I am sorry, so so) still and quivering
here in the cold

THE EDWIN FOX

I woke from my dream where I was a movie star, but one
of the ones known for her character. the neighbors

next door are making something out
of their house. they took out the porch, and

the columns that held the roof up are floating
suspended from the overhang. I can see

the line where the paint stops, where the weather
was kept from getting in by the surface

of the stoop. it is suddenly hotter, the weather,
and the self is more buoyant, too, my

breasts swelling, as if filled with gas, my brain uncomfortable
in its sediment. a ship can be a container for people. I saw one for inmates

heading to the antipodes. for coal and ale. for enslaved cane
workers destined to Cuba. even for women eventually, and then it was

a freezer hulk filled with sheep carcasses. when you go to sea, you have to bring
water. the Fox's metal boat skin, which is nothing

like wool, is blue and green and it touches the wood
skin below it. the ship lives in a low-budget museum, so I can touch it and get away

with it. the ship was a thing with masts. it sat in water too long, half
sunk in tides of salt. one part of the mast was always in, one

part always out, and then there was a middle part, always moving
in and out of it, soaking and drying. it let the water come to it and then

the air come to it. a girl is swept to sea with one wave and then back
to deck on the very next. daily, for years. until there is no wood to come to.

the ship is a cave. the masts stalactites and stalagmites. the empty part,
which is air, hovers between the two. I can remake the tide with my eyes. and outside

here there are cherry trees next to each other, two of them, and I didn't know
they were cherry until I saw them

blooming and their branches reached out to one another. one petal
after one petal after too many petals. I missed the buds

just saw the trees for the first time when I was walking home and they were flowers
entirely. the wood gone.

WAX FLOWER

wax flower
five petals
ten stamens
leaving
small hardened fruit

flower wrapped in wax paper
five petals in a star
tin stain on the tablecloth
needle leaves pricks on a tab
let small hardening

wax lips on a flower   wax way and bye
a wax rind cools on the moon peel
and your name in the seeds—
small hardened letters poke from
chintzy fruit

by my needle kiss left

VISITATION

in the dream where I don't know
she is dead, she comes to me and I talk to
her about none of the things I want to
talk to my dead mom about. she traces an oval on a wax tablet.
asked about scale, she answers, the landscape just happened
to be the size of the frame. the visit is shallow or it finds
depth in the places we don't talk. we spend our time
walking over a field robed in cotton. sound moves
fastest in solids. faster in water than
in air. breath, it turns
out, is the slowest medium, and the words I
have are thick in their churning over. the materials
only few and so thin. we share a food
between us. I want
to have a child if only to clarify the image
she weaves—a suit that happens
to be just the size of my body. I sew a shadow
to each petal with a curved
quilting needle. amplitude
and speed, I am telling you, are unrelated. my name
is the last name my mother refused
to change. so as not to lose you, the hospital
lists your name with your mother's on your
baby wristlet. this
life is a repetition that knows
no bounds, tracing a tablet into a waxing
oval that spirals outward. seed of a
seed sowing itself into the ground. this name
just happens to be the size of the concept growing. gesture
is a manner of carrying a body, and space opened
to sky in the recess of her breathing as she
came up from the water, a film

breaking over the ridge of her nose. moving between
water and air, the exhalation faster than her body, I remember
she is dead.

              a tree is taken from its halo of
needles. a red candle drops an oval around itself
onto cloth.

SHEDDING

I show you the slenders
elbow crooks   feather ridges in new fat
blood surfaces blue through the pales
tongue blisters the air in a cut
spit sheen on aluminum
my sternum, a boned shift
lingering filigree radios over
dunes capped, subtracted I
press to a bridge, you bruise your rib
a pulsing vertebra carves an *s*
sounding for depths
starting fires in quiet stacks of thatch
chord circle crease
the body weaves a braid of oilmuscle   longer
skin peels and makes a wind sock
the thinnest parts the last to touch
as you turn away, the blades of your back blip
the ghost detaches   floats from the tail
a plastic bag outruns you in a parking lot

SIDELONG: TREATISES

the moon is bigger, but I am pretty
sure we are both celestial objects, carved out of the dark by the sun.

snow keeps snowing, renewing itself. I wake in the morning
to find it fresh again, a pristine crystal.

the thing about a cliff is the cliffside, otherwise
it would remain a carpet unfurling in front of you, forever.

the voice becomes the trailing thing in the
forest, tree branches holding to a sound, and I am reminded

last night I dreamt of balconies and expensive art and
my sister lying atop embroidered linens in a hotel room.

with regard to the light from the sun, we have a side,
which is to say we have two, a shadowed and a bright, the light follows

the sloping surface hanging long down the
body, the world a robe, more glistening than I thought

it could be. I am a surface considered from a particular direction. what are you
good for. you see me as a blue thing, through rose liquid, open my duration, unfurling
                                                                    forever.

the snow shudders and seizes. when the branches are overcome the
birds startle, breaking open their wings to make the winter flower.

side, long, deep; spoken of a roof. heard of
my way of sleeping, sighing like I like. I drink into it. a marbled pool.

PILE

n. a dart, shaft, or arrow. *Obs.*

my mother's ring in its box,
on a shelf, in a room
what a box, velvet-lined, what
a ring, a racket to cut
its glimmer comes for me on my
singlet shade
and you dress me in crystal
my ears pierced with sound

n. the plumage or feathers of a bird,
    esp. the downy plumage; the downy part of a feather.

not the steering vane. the softer
plume for warmth. a scent's apparition. partition favors breaking.
eggs. ochre sap. wax seal on a plum. stem. polly's pocket.
champagne flute. crown. tension hitting a bank.
fray to fiber. promise? pattern. necks. news.
down. downing. downy chick.
covenant. chicka *dee dee dee*

n. the raised surface or nap on a fabric

quiet clutter quiet clutter
gently purple moss
velvet has loops has plied thread

achieving lush a line
and then another   linelush
brought above the surface and cut
spreading fiber to fruit

have fruit do you have   lush
how deep   can you press
into the skin
running my hand
in one direction marking

a scape requires
more than one
color of thread put a strand of
tinsel in your nest   a strand
tensile in your proof

drive my bundles
to the junkyard   bring
kerosene for a
lusher   flame

n. a heap, stack, or mass.

fustian therefore smoke wherefore fustian loop fustian
fustian here for heretofore loop softness fustian fustian
shimmer a lusher fustian texture fustian tumor a looser
forthwith thread fustian have I my fustian location fustian
mass quadrant have I fustian found my fussy loop to cut

v. trans.　to fasten with nails. *Obs.*

　　　　　　　　to fix or drive (a stake, etc.) in the ground. *Rare.*

my mother planted things
sank them into
earth. round forms.
bulbs. a supplementary
warp makes the ground
softer. velvet. she wasn't planted
preferred to be burned and cut
open. scattering over root,
　　　　　dirt caught in a dead drift.

MACHINE

the fabric of the world or universe and I mean
to hold it lightly, my fingers extending within the
bud to pull out an aphid small enough not to eat
truly truly a lick of sustenance from the dust and my
machine is supple and I will hold
it as I mean *the part of a flail that strikes the grain,* a protein
taken in threshing. the sea fabric meets the sky fabric
a threaded graft, the warmth reaching *the depth of earth*
that may be thrown up at once with a spade which is to say a spit
of land.
        you lie in the garden.
I watch your beard hairs grow to match
the chrysanthemum. as they ignite in the shine
off the glass of the water, the day becomes
too dazzling for mirrors. a ray
splits and I catch it *a stripe, a king,*
a chopped straw. my unfurling is
a luxurious arrangement. I let the pink russet and ripen. when I say, finish
I mean *to come, to end, to give completeness or perfection.*
I mean the light swallowing
a small piece of gold or silver leaf.

OFFICE OF THE HOLY FACE

There are species of abandonment   spectral fringe   hot error

wave me in   to the vacancy pending

scene of   buoys   untethered   floating

     to find one and an other   huddled on the ocean field   a school of

rustling   over depth   gathering

     pretty luck   glutted shot-tied

     I want a carcass to sing   fever pitch

to me in golden-hour light   the body revives

made a song tunnel   I am tired   of precious boys

of my mother's ghost halving   a limpid shiver primed

aloft   the blade of hera plow tilling

 its own ash

     hers a haunting

    having nowhere   to wander to

     I need   that good relic

a portrait possessed by a flickering   tallow-light

an exercise to think   her body   dead and alive

saw a seedpod opening   its papery mouth to reveal black teeth

and thought of fall falling   a horizon

ship hulls cut through a glassy distortion of the night sky as chains of aqueous mountains sit dumb below, covered in underwater. the first feast days of saints were those of martyrs. St. Agnes prayed to protect herself from rape, and God responded by collapsing her prepubescent body and covering it with shivering hair.

underneath the water, the brunette pelage appears oily, like undulating strands of kelp. Agnes sets one of the aqueous mountain ribs for supper, laying out forks and knives among the heavy water and bottom rubble. each stone rocked back and forth by fingerlike currents, touched repeatedly till smooth, shaped, the stones are, as the inside of mouth, perfect for holding between the palate and tooth and cheek, a sound caught still. it is dark and blue in this place so deep. under incredible pressure the calendar days fold into one another, all the saints eat together at once over the ash-choked surface. they feast on jellied fish on toast and almond-shaped pebbles for good digestion. Teresa points to the crevice she first envisioned as Hell. Peter touches Agatha's breasts as if glass, unbelieving in the miracle of his own healing. they all hold scars of their earthly trials, all have navels. out of deference to the stuffed quiet, I dare not mention the word, an unspoken made round enough to hold us here in hunger.

VISITATION

my mother   sitting at a table opening

bread   her fingers moving with a bitter

hiccup. the table shines under the torn food

she breaks open for

me and she pulls a   hyacinth from the center—

her breeding seed, counting each piece

my eyes shine with bluepetals and

she   asks me if

my brothers are all right if   my sister

is still afloat in the giant sad sea

of losing a lover to heroin.

            She asks of her own

eyes, a vision of a voided ceiling

leaving no hem to wipe up our puke

no string for our hair.

she asks me nothing of myself   only

if I am eating and I say

enough.

if darkness is to lightness as weight is to lightness
a hallway is two windows connected by a tube
or two squares of light surrounded by heavy dark.
darkening weight. ink weaves into matter.
if darkness is absorption the light swallows into
my matter. if coldness is heat
leaving, everything around the darkness is cold. my
pain is alone. and the darkness
is heatful. and to be left out in the light
is the arrival of snow. a snow night would be
bright with crystal. my submission would be to be
light with edges. a body of heat builds
to its brightness. as brightness is lightness
reflected, the sheen, a surface slickened. ink opens
in water. shallow is little depth, undeepening.
shadow is unlightening. the shadow in shallow
is slight. a pleasure is a hurtness coming
and leaving at once. it is a heaving
window collected by a tube. the shallow
in shadow is light. coming through a stocking. silken heat. silky
plaything. my coming apart will be a ray unneat
in its depth. the sand moves if wave
is to particle as light is to light.

THREAD SPLIT BY A NEEDLE [DESERTS]

tasted arrival in the eye of the storm   infinitely edged fractal miracle   hum-

of my usual attenuation are you of something   bigger or smaller   than a

seems to be my only option   tired of the   dreary-gone-dolly address

dog a still water   minnows beneath   the see-thru-me ice   flicking bubbles

a loom   -ing   threaded   into my woman-suit   suited

free bacon   I am still unclear   of my   commitment   to this

a rule   path to   follow and resurrect   across two boards drum-killing tizzy machine a line long   enough to convince me

self   making tinctures from the reigning atmosphere

elect   something with a tooth in it   of the bark   of the

how many hatchlings do you   have on the line? body

sweated   swear to break no eggs swear to eat the cruelty-

lengthening   it becomes me   anyway

nailed   an ex-   really

sill-ledge

to sip the milk of a reverse night sky

what was the last thing I gave up

 I am

that hot feeling

center counter chorus

capsule dipped in light   currently

sheath opening   the syncopated

have you seen a wing span

like a lasso   careful not to

framed

I am placed   upon

an X atop the heart of the thing, hoping

cheeks billowing

to make room for the new self

brooding

a nursing niggling creature thing

candy-coated, snap in the teeth

pulse through a wire

 v of geese   unstrung

a dress lifted   through a window

touch the ground

famous

I am your   fitful furniture

[desert]

moonish
everything naked without its shade

[irregular desert]
punctuated heights, a candle
of a rock formation—
its flame a quivering shadow
body a bell, ringing me   ravenous cavernous

next year will I write
next year will I write
          a new poem just like this
one with   the same swell and retirement of depth

tracing over a   this word and then a this
the mark
lost between this dune and its twin in the
double desert

SOUND (SWOONING)

all at once
blooms scale a
clipped
delight, delicate to consider
eggs in the tongueleaf
fair-haired nettles
gowned in such
hot hot cloud, hunger.
I am looking for honey
joy, nonesuch
kittening, unfolding the
lark's spurring tongue in a
mewing mouth. de-
nature the
openings—take
pattern to crevice and
quake. a
radio storm riveting
shakes to
tracked earth, sticky
uvulas—
very anatomy, all of a sudden, to be
wrist-tied with
xanthan gum
yes, thicker, please and
zipped.

NOCTURNE

barely moon and
the thread is fainter
      every cloud touch
I imagine you
fucking me
but also you telling me
no your mouth goes
still and discarding

being inside a love   so great
I never existed   watching smoke
      drift from pink to mauve
in a cold glass room

the mood deletes
the air I could   find
to speak   the shadows

duning best

there between the sight and my eyes
I know which
shapes the shapes must be

PEONY

the buds will open, or
if it is Tuesday, and you are still in California
will they remain
buds, willing to be but no
you to witness the unfolding. will they
unfold from their budshells, or huddle
as beetles, crimp wing
shriveling down
to a nut—
the weight of petals, cellulose
ribboning and suffocating
lace, muffle and ply. may I
may I breathe here—will you—
no   no breath
in a room filled with petals.

ants crawl over the pink
nectar-searching,
they do not hurt the blossoms
nor do the blossoms need them
to open but I comfort
in the tracing of pale surfaces
to inners and
the ants eating away fibrous tissues
unletting
the waxy string that holds all of it
together, and then the petals will
come undone
and fall as hair de-furling from a knot
held so long and plaited,
texture pressed, pleasured
and lowered, you pulled the tie
from my hair with desperate
trying to smell
me all at once each cell
in collision in comet
a ruffling of folded tin
crumpled newspaper that writhes and
unfolds in flame

54

extinction in blue smoke—

                              but if you are
are still in California on Tuesday, still
it is impossible to know as the peonies
are not yet blooming
yet full to the nubbins, the very sepal
tired of holding
all the petals that must be inside, how many
numbers are no answer
as they separate one
from the next, not the number
that I need
which is a pleated thing swelling along interstice
to lower the thread between
a you and an I
searching
something that helps me count
the time we have
been together and the swelling
of the time we must be
apart, so that we may
may we just now, be it
that we have these peonies
the peonies in their fullness make me
want, want to get married
in May.

VISITATION

when she arrives
to my sleep, I think
how small, your shoulders and then
my mother tells me
she has read my poems.
she liked the one about
peonies because she likes
poems about the end
of the world, she says.
the poem is about peonies.
still, it is the one
she wants
framed with its secret,
a covert destruction
invisible even to me.
she wants it
in a glass box that gives
the illusion
of hovering, as if the poem
has no weight—
not even the small heft
of a sheet
of paper. she
doesn't want anything
to touch it.

LUSH/ /BRINK

I go to bed to see the light drop, bloom
behind my me—the eyelid films—then cease
in leaves. Watch petals pinking woolen from a loom,
we touch the brimming texture, feeling crease
release to spring, to rays. A purpling croons
below the sheet, a dewy-eyed increase—
a shine in two, outbreaking, wreathes the room.

You wear a crown of little doves, creased
to thorny beaks, I stuff your mouth, gray plume
pillows and floats   over. As if to lease
a coin, in debt from us to us, love fumes
and makes it soon (too moon, too soft) a feast
of glowing discs upon my teeth, and resumes—
touching and   released.

HYDRANGEA

I smell water in the air here, it's water the air here
that fills a bubble   so unlike a diamond
to return to the air a feeble stone in its
sound   chirped through
vibrate and empty
so unlike a diamond
you carved on the bed   so far
are mine in an earth place
radiolocate the marveling body in
clear water over   clear water another cellophane
layer and the ocean below the ocean is dark
somehow   I've touched only
the first ten feet true how this particle
and the far particle are
the same in time and so outside
of it   I changed
my density changed my
mind for a plenty and deeper likeness
the blossoming multiple
loosening capsule
an excellent fiber
the sea-den is wrapped in velvet
you've welcomed the gentle thing to eat it
baby ocean   baby-fur-foam liken to
a quiet sort
absorbed in its saltshine   the untold swarms from a
cup shape of a seed filling
many-headed   the diamond pulls a face
from a crown

58

walking home from fireworks   /a hunting light comes over us

people tree-tall   /casting their darknesses, collecting

speed and pattern, dispersing again   /

we sweat into the night   /alcohol-slicked and roiling

sickle-shaped mandible, carved runnel   /the ribbon is a gash

/the shine, spit

flooded like someone running   /we follow each other's backs

lines between each slab of   /sidewalk brim with grass

sparklers humming their static   /how much soil there must be

another greenery encroaching   /the trees cut-out of their shadows

a diorama kept a specimen, a spine   /of the sharp scent, untethered

the sound that filled out the sky   /unhinged the cherry branches, each flesh bud holds a stone   /

jab the stirrup, the pain   /you won't own is yours

        you are on the un-   /dead side of the river

THE CLAUDE GLASS [A CONVEX TINTED MIRROR]

catalog. art. 1

*box of cherry, inlaid with a thin band of lemon
horn frame, pleasing and useful for viewing
eclipses, clouds, landscapes, &c.*

catalog. art. 2

"Objects are not presented with that depth, that gradation, that rotundity of distance, if I may so speak, which nature exhibits; but are evidently affected by the two surfaces of the mirror, which give them a flatness, something like the scenes of a play-house, retiring behind each other. The convex-mirror also diminishes distances beyond nature, for which the painter should always make proper allowance. Or, to speak perhaps more properly, it inlarges foregrounds beyond their proportion. Thus, if you look at your face in a speculum of this kind, you will see your nose magnified. The retiring parts of your face will appear of course diminished."
—William Gilpin, *Remarks on Forest Scenery and Other Woodland Views,* 1791

catalog. art. 3

ankles in gray water   fingers in   gray

water   the self water   a non-portrait

     a lake in the palm

features retiring, of course tiring

compact

the clamshell holding its own

split   in my pocket   pearl-less

catalog. art. 4

varieties of -mancy ["divination by"]

      catoptromancy ["mirrors"]
      tainomancy ["the foil backing of mirrors"]
      palmomancy ["thick ink in the hollow of the hand"]
      perspiromancy ["salt trails"]
      cartomancy ["cards"]
      hydromancy ["water"]
      nephomancy ["clouds"]
      cucharomancy ["curve of the spoon, speculum of this kind"]
      botanomancy ["leaves, herbs, and tree branches"]
      retinomancy ["the reflective film of the eyes"]
      respiromancy ["intake of breath"]
      sophiomancy ["loving, left"]
      photomancy ["death masks"]

catalog. art. 5

sharkskin, not marble but obsidian
rounded, shaped as the arc
of a billowing circle, not a sheet
not the film that drapes flat
by table-casting *the secret*
of applying quicksilver and tin a tain
of another color *a particular stone*

catalog. art. 6

a ghost

      of the place over my

shoulder. my my   what color

are the bands of amaranth   pendulous. the showy

hollyhocks brighten their own

faces. a pesky picture   always jutting

flits just   out of frame   the foliage

still growing   the trees frighten

as they move   giving

      the threat of a branch

splayed over a body   a shadow

across a face, eyes closed

brindlevision

     a body   of water

    in hand

THE KIND OF THING
at Hearst Castle

I stole a lemon from the bower on the hill
when I was sure the maintenance workers
whizzing about in their golf carts wouldn't see.
the tapestry in the castle shows strange
bees, bird-shaped, their wings
feathered rather than veined. the tiles
in the castle show the games
girls play. the ceiling is Spanish
and maroon, smoked two shades darker by blubber lamps and
after-dinner cigars. the workers restore it at night with
the infinite strokes of oversized cotton swabs.
in the garden, there is a marble basin, the size
of a child's bath, filling with water from a green
PVC hose.

I like film because it lets me see a time lapse of
a mushroom and I can watch as the cap lets down its lace
netting to the forest floor, and I imagine my fingers are small
enough to fit through the holes—I like that I can't
check. I like my own eyes for the snow, I like my own eyes for seeing
the zebras on the estate. the object is the resource. it's the kind of thing
you've stolen even if you've paid for it. I don't want
to speed up or slow down, I just want
to be and let the snow decide if it will
cover me. the zebras are even
harder to spot in a dusting, their stripes a burnt
brown like the California hills. I like
to imagine a white peacock strutting over
the lawn where there is none.

we decide not to stop

for the sunset, I watch the raspberry cloud not moving even

as we are trying to drive it by. the sunset follows,

eyes in a masterpiece, the light is still

changing, and I can see the night

approaching a velvet band in the

modulated darkness, as if my head were

underwater and I needed a place

to rest, so I bend my body in two

and let the fat on my hips float me

to the surface.

VISITATION

cows so black they are purple
nosing among bristles dry
enough to break ochre
through troughed snow,   thinning
all the colors gone matte

no reflection, no sheen

my mother
this morning
pulling back the lashes
of those eyes,
big and brown, fearful
she breathes out and sees it,   her lung
ghosted in front of her
dissipating in the print
of the cows' mouths

cut from the picture, a space sewn

she looks
at their teeth and at the plastic tags
in their ears, bends to touch
the hooves, pulls a tangerine
from hard soil and opens it,   gives
me the pith for my gums,   and keeps
the waxy ribbon for herself

it's dream, thick sadness,
"heaping infinite upon infinite"

I align four rosettes in cardinals
red beacons to true the needle
the fence fills with milky glass—icicles
wind shoals hollow   north

everything still less. the fanfare for the vicissitudes of sitting
in the shadow of the coming
wave. which salinity my
salinity, bring me into the salt—
the water's never blue when you're under it,
mine is a sapphire leaving.
EBB talks about passion as being prone,
covered in seaweed-like hair.
"self is put away" overcome in the golden mist,
be the material of the musical jolt.
I'd like a metaphor without godcum,
but I get it—the seed thing—external
figures always easier, available to the tips
of the brain. do you have the voice
of your age? do you like
what you have? I like dunes
more than diaphragms, the mist the golden
residue of a continual erosion. it was
glass, and then it was glass, and then smaller
glass. pieces of. time rubbed it into something un-
dangerous. what is the scale of
a voice pumped into a dune, vibrato keeps the fine
powder elevated, a cloud for our inhalation

INFINITY IN TWO SIZES

a mist over a field

over, distinct from, the clear film between

the mirror line reflecting two depths unfathomable

upon first and second sight

seeds in the ground, the ground, opaque extending

the snow above the field, and then

on the top of the head of the field, weighing the

needle grasses. an intermittent gathering

as the cold saturates, the surface

guards the whole crystal   snow

until covering this inch, and this inch, and this

my line that begets lines

the seeds nosing out into earth

from my place in the grass the stems are taken

over by the air, into the cloud, then, the blades *flicker tick*

rays of light plus 1 still in shine

the fields I draw with my index finger

the glass box my breath escapes

red wax melted, and dropped to seal

my petite infinity, his also, peaked

through the apple branches

floating along a sheet tacked to a wall for watching
film, I found the sensation

                         hovering. below me,
always again. I was small when I was a child
and I saw the clouds from above for the first
time, from an airplane, I thought—this is my
grand revelation, let it be recorded: far enough
above the ground, an expanse of surface separates
you from the rest of the breathing everyone

       you arrive   again

underwater—

before the airplane the tops of clouds were
congeries gathering in the void above so many
earth-bound heads. the film of the bubble fills
with the image of a   thought. more like a
dissipating shadow.   as my eyes follow the
black movement   of a ligature. more like a
sparkler writing   my name through a dark-
ness. the character   refuses to materialize
into anything. but   itself—but the cloud. but
the letter. but   the lichen patches that make
a chartreuse   path of the riverbed. but again,
the cloud. I   must insist on it. the top of it.
is it a ball of cotton still quiet with its thorn. if
I turn it over in my hand to look at the facet
that faces away from me do I find

                        a mirror reflecting
color. the gray of my eye in a fat, solid block or
a gradation of white moving into mauve as
along the fleshy petal of the saucer magnolia. is

it a dust
-less window for viewing the
burning stars beyond
even this big firmament.
could I stand on it. would I sink
in to my knees before I came
upon my mother and her Mary,
who I can't believe in,
how long would I stand before I
too was enveloped in the cold of the
airborne particle. how much longer
must she be dead
before she doesn't
recognize my face.
it's a needle still
the cloud I have
been insisting
on the image that
I don't want to see
the image I want kept
clouded and forever
far from the crystalline
such a definition.
always, again.
a needle.

MIDDLE OF A CLOUD, NO TELESCOPE. (SENTIMENTAL)

it is the thing about clouds that they look
like other things.
when I see a cloud I think of other
clouds. its cloud siblings, its contiguous
particles unbelonging
to anyone. they coalesce in a wave and
pulse in and out of each
other's bodies.

I hear clouds
are never
not moving.
I can imagine sitting in the middle of the cherry trees
(blooming white at this very moment) and the insects
that would crawl over my forearms. do ants ever sleep.

if my mother met me now, I would be half
of a stranger. she would be unchanged. maybe
blurrier. she sits, a mist in a glass case.

she has seen enough
cherry blossoms. even
in death, each new
year they are white.

the sensation of ants crawling over the
peonies, always again, the petals become
the skin thin on the wrists. they feed on my sweat,
they feed on my sweet. the pink
I choose
for my thoughts is
sparkling.

ALL MOVEMENT MIMICS OTHER MOVEMENT

Small birds that flit
between bushes in December make me
remember movement
as it could be:
a quick sparkle or a hurried arrow through the snow,
hanging baubles along the way.

I imagine a string suspended after each of the starling tails,
and soon the snowy airspace
fills

with a knot dense and beautiful.

It is the shape that ice takes in shallows:
shoals of featherlike fibers
encased in glass
where the grass crosses itself
and pokes up amid snow

FLORIOGRAPHY
a translation

dianthus

myosotis bindweed myosotis,
bindweed viola bind
digitalis, weed
chicory. amaranth
bind bellis perennis bind
weed bellis perennis bellis perennis—

bindweed chicory, weed
amaranth bind chicory. viola,
tricolor, collinsia weed
sedum.

wild geranium bind ranunculus, weed
amaranth viola
canina bindweed petasites,
weed convulvullus
weed wild carrot, weed crocus
versicolor bind
prunus padus,
plains coreopsis, bind
viola tricolor.

sweet william

forget me not in the scorpion grass,
my heart's ease is dressed
in lady's glove, fastened
bachelor's button. the prince
feather wakes the day's eyes for just
the sight of daisy daisy—

and so, I'm nursing hurtsickle, become your
love-lies-bleeding in a bluebottle. love,
in idleness, my innocence turned
to stonecrop.

a dove's foot prates the lesser celandine, as you
my velvet heath
dog hung with butterbur,
proffer me the devilgut
in lace, in a cloth
of silver and I
cough up the birdcherry,
a golden tickseed, and watch
my heart   cease.

FLOOD SEASON

I draw you out on a bed, and look for your cancers. I press above your hipbone, a step from your navel. Under my fingers your gut tenses to muscle, full in the place where one cleans a fish. Coiled iridescence smells like iron, and I know with the right attention your blood-slicked innards would unfold easy. Perched above you my breasts are heavy like ballasts rigged for opening velvet, oil lanterns, animal carcasses, or even stones draping thatch. I knew you best falling out of bed for the first time, how your nipples glimpsed then shied away in your redressing. We go outside, and you pick up lake water in your hands, consider its weight as it splits over your knuckles. With the liquid let out, the diatoms and microcorals settle to a film— stack and pile, shift and dig. When we get home I clean your nails in a white basin. I watch particle follow particle down the sink. Under glass, lung tissue forms dyed clouds. It is an echo of the foam uncovered in autopsies of drowning victims: pink-aerated   cumulonimbus.

FEATHER   CRANE   SWARM

the ravine between the highway and the field   fills with smooth sumac
broken in the hand   it stains   leaves red
    on the palm
    my sister broke her   her baby tooth at the zoo
same three-year-old body   on the bluff at that parade watching floats across concrete

    stepped in the fire ant   nest in her jelly sandals, with her small feet.
my mother stripped her of   her clothes of her terry suit too late   to save her the biting,
my sister still resents her   young nakedness   in a crowd   of people of insects,   she was

    rough on her body.   we have always   been rough on   our bodies.

spit shone from our foreheads, ashed crosses smear and sweat out   from clay soil,
we didn't want any baptisms,   didn't want any   blessings   until we were left

without benediction for   our sick body leaving us, my   mother's hands puckering
done drinking   and her limbs the first to go cold. the blood stayed   to her belly.

    when she died,   the nurse dressed her in   a clean dress
      and I lay by her simple body,
noplasticnotubes body   cotton and skin as the muscles relaxed   from their living
    let her fluid go   stain her   pelvis

pigment swelling   clay soil   earth   to   clouds take a color swarming
    reflect the brimmed   arsenals below   plants rusting,   all that iron in the cloth tooth

green holding white birds,   cotton settling down

    of her death dress

VIOLET PORTRAIT

subtle gradient

lavender purple lilac purple

grape hyacinth brushed mauve

soft teasel, heathered indigo

an iris dilating, deepening, lu-pining

bruising pansies, tingeing hydrangea

but

      the neon crocus
      knocks your skirt up

VISITATION

I enter an apartment filled with someone else's things. We lie on the bed and talk of the luxury of clean sheets. She starts stripping the mattress. I jostle to avoid the small birds of her hands pecking the creases. When she finishes she folds up and tucks herself into a ceramic basin smaller than a loaf of bread. I watch her as she turns into idling water, her belly translucent as the edges of her nails and no voice box to speak of.

SHORN

mine is a self I wish I didn't have

to look at, a head bobbing neckless

on a heath ocean. waves disrupt reflection,

I say, for a bloom born of

a time of temperance, your ticking is lush.

which is to say, I miss afternoons detonating

in the growing sound of insects. limes on the lip.

by the real ocean, scotch broom

covers the path, too much to move through

without rubies beading a scratch. it's just blood. the hedge overgrows

itself, is filled with spiders cottoning

the barbs, their own catching mechanism, the silk reels

in on itself to its slack droplet. I am the directionless

vertebra digging into a lavender sandbar. such lovely. when

we were new you brought something

out of me, a coil that got fatter as it emerged. a sponge taken from

its plastic pill, and let to soak

A chalice made of ostrich shell. The audio guide tells me that ostriches are symbols of virgin birth, that 18th-century thought told of how the plumed animals laid their eggs in desert sand and left the sunlight to hatch chicks (yield one feathered baby Jesus).

A jamboree of furniture and nonsense. The embroidery is too delicate for winter temperatures, so instead the elbows of the cloth are crossed with the knees of the table. The glass decoupaged with orange vacuoles and insect antennas.

Amber. No-nonsense sunlight and hardened tears. It is just of jutting resin. With ivory ankled in the door handle. The toes of stones stand on pedestals. Pedestals shaped like pomegranates and winter fruits.

A platter mosaic of mother of pearl arranged to imitate wings. A wing-ed shivering thing dipped in oyster.

Things come easy if you ask politely. I may give you a jewel from my collection of salt and nail polish. Your arms are jumbled when you reach for me: such is the nature of phenomenal movement.

n. Hearing; the sense of hearing. *Obs.*

Song? A little one. Here. I'll leave
you some spare rows. In a pile. Smoking.
You see it? Taste it. Pick it up with your
jaw joint, your flecked language.

Lay the air. Gray wings agitate to a foam.
Fighting? Frightened. Bickering salt. Bittering
butter. Hot poppy. Fire color. Which
variable pigment. Modulated tone. White note.

Burnshimmer tonguing the lobe.
Buzzing. Brandish. Flammable. My mouth is
flammable. Ears itchy.
My teeth acid eating. Pflaumen—
plums plums plums. How sweet the
cake   to be loved by you.

n. Art, craft, cunning. *Obs.*

falling light checks the stiff silk

knock the polish to get the bubbles out

the sepal houses a spitting beetle

n. A border, hem, bordering strip. *Obs.*

light	smatters	second	instant
what	joy/	joy jolly	hello
I /	need	some	metric
pressure	pleasure?	pleasure/	please/
pleasure	if you	want	some
pleased /	pretty/	pretty girl	give
me	some	pleasure	pleases
did you	make it	with	
your	mouth	this/	carved
needful		a thing	you
can't hold		coming	

n. The careening or inclination of a ship to one side. *Naut.*

we loved for a long time.
we loved for a long time and then
we didn't   love for a bit and we loved
bitter for a time that wasn't the love we loved
before but now a vacant flavor—
he has those curls. he has the body
that we used to share in his bed. we loved for
a long time. how long has the time
been since we loved, how long have
my arms become in having
someone new
how long is a loving thing in this
how long how hollow my loving
we loved   for a time I longed
I longed for a time to
love like   I love, I longed
for a long time for the new
body I'm touching, the one
I have in my bed, and he left me too
lonely and I am longing after
longing for a for a long time a lingering
longing I am waiting I am longing
for a long time of loving
a long longing
my listless
how long
in this cavern of small loves
my longing sheet
my blue blue blandishment
the jet that leaves a white
letter in the air

multiple blossoms on a skein
unfolding in
a succession of uniform rhythms.
each blossom is the
soon-to-be
of the blossom above it.
those at the base are
withered, brown
the top buds not even
flowers yet
the one in the middle just starting
to go papery at its edge.
the day unthreads, and then the next
day unthreads.

all cannot be full at once. the olfactory sense
develops fully by the end of the first trimester.
the lover I have will never know my mother. the
child I don't have will never know my mother.
they won't know to miss (as in, long for) the
dark cuticle at the top of her front tooth, the one
she always hid in pictures. I only saw it when she
flossed, leaning over the sink and pulling back
her lips for a better look. I feared my mouth
turning such a color. was it the right tooth or
the left? I have no body to check; the obituary I
wrote is elision. if you lose the baby late enough,
your milk still comes in, and no one to eat it. I'm
confusing bodies. it's my mother I've lost, not
my baby. my lover I am waiting to lose. so enters
the wanting. the worry. of identifying my love in
the days after he dies, and no face to be found.
day-old newborns find their mothers by scent,
sniffing out the milk-soaked flesh with their eyes

closed. which of his lower back muscles has the mole? mole (of the skin, not of the earth) in Spanish is *lunar*. as in, of the moon. my color will come and then leave, leaving me too fragile to smell.

the light that shines through milk glass is red-orange, the material itself blue-green. the youtube time lapse of a silkworm I watch in July while I am home alone in my underwear because it is too hot and I am trying not to move, begins with eating. the silkworms, their searching faces lost within circumcised heads the color of ivory, follow the bone of a mulberry leaf, crawling over each other's soft-fleshed bodies. to be honest in seeing them, I am still in love with linen drying in sunlight, the residual heat the night folds into itself. the worms chew the leafmeat to its vein. once gorged, a single larva separates and builds its cocoon from the outside in, constructing a curtain over an anchoring thread suspended from one branch or leaf and attached to the next.

before I was sitting in my underwear, I imagined this. I imagined wrong the cocoon as a mummy and the moth-pupa the subject of my own fantasies of an incremental pressure that begins with the milky film enveloping the prey of a spider, the process accumulating as fat around a body. I dreamed of the inflation of a cocoon that would build outward. instead the worm undertakes an exercise in constructing its own restriction. claustrophilic, he begins in a sheer, voluminous tent, he sticks his rear out of the structure and shits for the last time. I gasped aloud. how final it was, the wet goop drying to a black mulberry-shaped pellet as the tail retreats, and the construction continues. the walls become more and more like walls, layer upon layer thickening until the worm is inside a padded room without a door. the cocoon constricts, nearing opacity, and the weaving body within is increasingly obscured until it becomes white, a uniform mass, any shimmer of light or distinction in color the false fulfillment of a wish to see something still, moving. glitter in the scattered ash of fireworks. smoketrail/afterimage/premonition. at the moments of greatest observational pressure, desire seeps into perception. the excess is the stomach rising in the body's descent.

age is arresting. seeing the stilling of the worm to an opaque stasis (as finally it had nowhere more to move) was the very same as watching a chicken egg on a reel of film warming up, the shell blinking until the spool of the movie projector had reached the 24 frames per second required to bring forth a solid oval on the blooddark screen of my eye. the milk glass contains opacifiers that precipitate as crystals as they cool. salt rushes to the heat of my brain as I come to the sheet surface, and my sweat is the high contrast of the white petal with the purple center of the pepper flower. settling into my remainder.

VISITATION

We emerge from a drowned place, just she and I—
and she spits up foam. So it is water
we've been holding. I feel none of its movement.
I worry she will mistake me for a river stone, but she knows
the small hiccup I make before I sneeze. She knows
my Sunday smell. Grief for the grief I must give up. I blink
until my eyes become stones and reach—

She alights on the surface bevel
and preens the loose threads
from my sampler. She continues
pulling seeds from a stitched
rose, disintegrating to become

a nest.

FOR KIT KELLY (1951-2013)

I'll look for you at the shore.

Acknowledgements

Thank you to the readers and editors at the following publications where earlier versions of these poems first appeared:

"Top of a cloud, no airplane." and "Hydrangea," *Sugar House Review*

"Shorn," "All movement mimics other movement," and "Visitation" in *On the Seawall*

"Lash," *RHINO*

"The Claude Glass," and "Pile," *Tagvverk*

"Thread split by a needle [deserts]," and "Lush border/ distillation," *Denver Quarterly*

"Middle of a cloud, no telescope. (sentimental)," *Chicago Review* online

"Gladiolus stem," *Mississippi Review*

"Visitation," *Prelude,* under the title "Vision 3"

"Cataract," *Afternoon Visitor*

"Feather crane swarm," and "Infinity in two sizes," *Hubbub*

"age of decadence//sericulture//summoning spell," *The Bennington Review*

"Newly, rendered, truly," and "Office of the Holy Face," *The Columbia Review*

"The Visitation," Ugly Duckling Presse's *Second Factory*

"Floriography: A Translation," *Yalobusha Review*

"Machine," and "Lush//Brink," *Turbine/Kapohau*

"Hyacinth," and "I cannot live with You," *Radar Poetry*

"Flood season," and "Shedding," in *Bathhouse Journal*

How does one even begin to acknowledge the village that makes a book possible? A brief and incomplete census of my village:

Thanks to my family—nuclear, extended, and chosen, especially my siblings—Brian, Dan, and Fiona—I would not have survived without you

Fred Hoffer and Donna Rodger

Tierney Flaherty, Devon VanPatten

Owen, Ronan, Oliver

Don, Kyle, and Kevin Thornburg

my mentors and teachers— Elizabeth Anker, Josh Bell, Mercy Carbonell, Jae Choi, Elisha Cohn, Jonathan Culler, Jay Dickson, Peter Gilgen, Ellis Hanson, Nathalia King, Mark Levine, Jane Mead, Julie Phillips Brown, Prageeta Sharma, Lisa Steinman, Elizabeth Willis, Emily Wilson

friends, old and new— John Anspach, Alan Argondizza, Mal Argondizza, Omid Bagherli, Farah Bakaari, Dahlia Balcazar, Nicole Balin, Claire Barwise, Victoria Baugh, Nikki-Lee Birdsey, Karlee Rene Bowlby, Emily Brown, Rose Bryant, Emmett Buckley, Bwesigye Bwa Mwesigire, Marty Cain, Daniel Carranza, Lubabah Chowdhury, Catherine Clepper, Jean Colley, Ruth Corkill, Rocío Corral García, Justin Cox, Christina DeVillier, Sophia D'Ignazio, An Duplan, Eran Eads, Colleen and Mitch Erickson, Ariel Estrella, Jeannine Falino, Christina Fogarasi, Laura Francis, Ben Fried, Jay Gao, Rachel Gardner, Annelyse Gelman, Kate Gibbel, Violeta Gil, Maura Gingerich, Simon Goldstein, Derek Gray, Mïi Gunn, Kathryn Harlan-Gran, Thomas Helmers, Vivian Hu, Jane Huffman, Kirsten (Kai) Ihns, Charline Jao, Jack Jung, Miri Karraker, Benjamin Krusling, Emmy Kumar, Nathan Likert, Joshua Macey, Michael Martin, Graham Miller, Olivia Milroy Evans, Joseph Miranda, Phil

Montenegro, Alyssa Moore, Patty Nash, Julianne Neely, Sara Nicholson, Liam O'Brien, Bevin O'Connor, Maggie O'Leary, Molly Peacher-Ryan, Alyssa Perry, Alec Pollak, Catherine Polityllo, Jasmine Reid, Emmalea Russo, Walker Rutter-Bowman, Susannah Sharpless, Sara Stamatiades, Kristen Steenbeeke, Emma Steinkraus, Kyhl Stephen, Rosie Stockton, Jon Stout, Chelsea Thomeer, Richard Thomson, Dave Toffey, Tasia Trevino, Ryan Tucker, Kelsi Vanada, Sophia Veltfort, Jan Verberkmoes, Kina Viola, Devon Walker-Figueroa, Alicia Wright, Winniebell Xinyu Zong

mis amigas españolas—me abrazasteis cuando estaba sola—Mónica Saiz Urrez, Ana Isabel Blázquez Díez, Sheila Oliva Navarro, María Pilar Natalia Roldán Gutiérrez, Ana Ibáñez Aróstegui, Almudena Rivas Quirós, Ainhoa Lopez Aranburu, Blanca Martínez, Eva Vaquero

the folks at Copper Canyon Press in Spring of 2013, especially Joseph Bednarik and Victoria Poling

my workshops at Iowa from 2015 to 2017

Katie Hardwick-Smith, Clare Moleta, and Chris Price

Diana Khoi Nguyen, Lisa Bickmore, Lauren Callis, and Lightscatter Press—for seeing me with such care

my students

my Bryce, who keeps me tender and good

my mother, who is everywhere and nowhere

Notes

"I cannot live with You," page 20. Title is borrowed from the first line of Emily Dickinson's poem F 706.

"I want Abysses," pages 17 and 25. Title is borrowed from a piece of dialogue spoken by Milly Theale in Henry James's *The Wings of the Dove*.

"Cataract," page 27. The italicized epigraph is taken from the etymology section of the OED's entry "cataract, n." The subscripts throughout the poem track the various definitions of "cataract" given in the same OED entry.

"Worry," page 28. Subtitle is taken from the OED's definitions of "worry."

"Pile," pages 37-41. All subtitles are taken from the OED's definitions of "pile."

"Machine," page 42. Text in italics is borrowed from various OED entries.

"The Claude Glass [a convex tinted mirror]," pages 61-63. The poem takes its title from the small, convex, tinted mirror used in 18th and 19th century landscape painting and sketching. Artists and tourists used Claude glasses, the shape and size of makeup compacts and familiarly known as "black mirrors," to frame their surrounding environment and reflect it in painterly tones. The instrument's rendering of the natural world in a style reminiscent of the picturesque painting style of Claude Lorrain gave the glass its name, although there is nothing to suggest Lorrain ever used one to produce his work. The poem's italicized language is borrowed (rearranged, edited) text from *The Claude Glass* by Arnaud Maillet (Zone Books, 2004).

"Visitation," page 66. "heaping infinite upon infinite" is a quotation pulled from "Personal Narrative" by Jonathan Edwards, as cited by Susan Howe in *My Emily Dickinson*, page 45.

"Floriography," page 73. "Dianthus" is comprised of formal or scientific names of plants and permutations of the word "bindweed." In contrast, "Sweet William" is comprised of the common or folk names for those same flowers. All of the adjectives and nouns (not including pronouns) are common/folk flower names.

"List," pages 80-83. All subtitles are taken from the OED's definitions of "list."

When light encounters an object, it bends and scatters: as a form of energy, it passes through the air, then shifts and deflects in ways not entirely predictable. At Lightscatter Press, we seek to publish the work of writers whose writing diffracts as it meets the world, finding life and light in multiple mediums.

This book is set in Arno Pro and Rig Shaded
Cover design by Kayden B. Groves and Jem Ashton
Interior design by Jem Ashton
Printed on archival-quality paper

Kelly Hoffer is a poet and book artist.

Her poetry was recognized as a finalist for the National Poetry Series in both 2020 and 2021. She has taught literature and creative writing classes at Cornell University, Victoria University, and the University of Iowa. She holds an MFA in Poetry from the Iowa Writers' Workshop, and she is currently a doctoral candidate in Literatures in English at Cornell University. She will join the faculty of the Helen Zell Writers' Program at the University of Michigan in the fall of 2023.

Undershore is her first book of poems.